Escaping the Boy
My Life with a
Sociopath

Escaping the Boy
My Life with a
Sociopath

REVISITED

Paula Carrasquillo

To order additional copies of this book, contact:
Xlibris Corporation
1-888-795-4274
www.Xlibris.com
Orders@Xlibris.com
118285

Contents

DEDICATION

For . . .
My loving husband Jorge. Without his love, I may still be stuck in
the dungeon.
My son who is my personal superhero.
My mother who is my guardian angel.
My dad who tries to understand these things.
My stepfather who would have been proud of me.
My sisters and brothers who I love unconditionally.
My friends and family who supported and encouraged me every step
of the way.
And, of course, for all the silent victims wishing and hoping
their suffering will one day end.
Namaste.

"She wrote a book about a little boy who grows up to be a mean old sociopath. It's a story that resembles my upbringing."

~ The boy's actual words spoken under oath in a court of law and said in a sing-song, mocking voice, only a sociopath could master so well

Author's Preface

Do you know what it feels like to be locked up, placed in a dungeon of a partner's creation? If so, you're not alone. If not, pray you never do.

Abuse comes in many forms and affects many people in the victim's life. Emotional, physical, and sexual abuses are equally degrading and harmful. One is not better than the other or worse than the other. They are ALL abuse.

Twice, I have been a victim (and survivor) of domestic violence/ intimate partner abuse in my lifetime.

At the age of 18, I was physically abused by my boyfriend who was also 18. He beat me repeatedly and threatened my life in many ways. I was able to escape the relationship but never spoke about it and was determined NEVER to put myself in that type of danger in the future.

Twenty years later, at the age of 38, I found myself in another abusive relationship, but I didn't recognize it as abusive because he never assaulted me physically (at first); the abuse was verbal and emotional. The control was overwhelming, and the insidiousness of his abuse slowly took over me and nearly destroyed my spirit and faith in goodness.

Today, 18 months after escaping my second abusive relationship, I have vowed to speak. I cannot remain silent.

This story is an account of my second abusive relationship and is presented as a work of fiction in order to protect the innocent (and it also, unfortunately, protects the abuser). I am no psychologist, psychiatrist, or counselor, but through extensive research, reflection, and acceptance, I have come to the conclusion that my emotional (and escalating physical) abuser can only be explained and described as being a narcissistic sociopath.

Out of a moral responsibility and obligation to all victims and survivors who continue to suffer and struggle with making sense of their abuse, I am compelled to share my experience.

This man's dark nature and psychopathology insidiously penetrated my body, mind, and spirit until I was nearly convinced that I was the evil one. How? Projection, transference, and control; that's how.

I hope you enjoy this story and pass it along to your family, friends, others you love, and anyone you suspect is or has ever been a victim.

Abuse is control: emotional, physical, and sexual control. Just because there are no visible bruises, doesn't mean a person isn't suffering from abuse at the hands of another.

Paula Carrasquillo
August 21, 2012

Identifying Narcissistic Sociopaths

According to Dr. Martha Stout's book *The Sociopath Next Door*, sociopaths make up 4% of western society (Stout, 2010). That's about 1 in 25 people walking around among us without a conscience, without the ability to measure, or care to measure, the morality of their decisions and actions. Would you know how to identify a sociopath if you saw one, met one, started an intimate relationship or entered into a business contract with one? More than likely, your answer is *No*, because unlike what we read on the television news or see in Hollywood movies, sociopaths aren't just serial killers and murderers. Rather, they are members of our communities who we would never suspect of evil or wrong doing and who seamlessly blend into society with the rest of us. How? Through lies, manipulations, and more lies.

In romance, narcissistic sociopaths often appear too good to be true. They are charming, agreeable, and engaging. The narcissistic sociopath loves (or seems to love) everything about you. He (or she) hooks you. Then he breaks you. His emotional abuse is VERY subtle. The victim may not know she is being victimized until it is nearly too late.

Although not all narcissists are sociopaths, all sociopaths are narcissists (Stout 2010). Therefore, if you can identify a narcissist, you're a step closer to being able to recognize a sociopath. Below is a definition of narcissistic personality disorder (NPD) and list of narcissistic traits taken directly from the website of Dr. Sam Vaknin, author of *Malignant Self-Love*. (If you know someone who fits at least 5 or more of these traits, a psychiatrist would easily diagnose him as having NPD, one step closer than the rest of us to being a sociopath.)

The DSM-IV-TR defines Narcissistic Personality Disorder as "an all-pervasive pattern of grandiosity (in fantasy or behavior), need for admiration or adulation and lack of empathy, usually beginning by early adulthood and present in various contexts," such as family life and work.

- Feels grandiose and self-important (e.g., exaggerates accomplishments, talents, skills, contacts, and personality traits to the point of lying, demands to be recognized as superior without commensurate achievements);
- Is obsessed with fantasies of unlimited success, fame, fearsome power or omnipotence, unequalled brilliance (the cerebral narcissist), bodily beauty or sexual performance (the somatic narcissist), or ideal, everlasting, all-conquering love or passion;
- Firmly convinced that he or she is unique and, being special, can only be understood by, should only be treated by, or associate with, other special or unique, or high-status people (or institutions);
- Requires excessive admiration, adulation, attention and affirmation—or, failing that, wishes to be feared and to be notorious (Narcissistic Supply);
- Feels entitled. Demands automatic and full compliance with his or her unreasonable expectations for special and favorable priority treatment;
- Is "interpersonally exploitative", i.e., uses others to achieve his or her own ends;
- Devoid of empathy. Is unable or unwilling to identify with, acknowledge, or accept the feelings, needs, preferences, priorities, and choices of others;
- Constantly envious of others and seeks to hurt or destroy the objects of his or her frustration. Suffers from persecutory (paranoid) delusions as he or she believes that they feel the same about him or her and are likely to act similarly;
- Behaves arrogantly and haughtily. Feels superior, omnipotent, omniscient, invincible, immune, "above the law", and omnipresent (magical thinking). Rages when frustrated, contradicted, or confronted by people he or she considers inferior to him or her and unworthy (http://samvak.tripod.com, retrieved August 21, 2012).

Once it's clear you're dealing with a narcissist, go through the following list to see if the narcissist is also a sociopath. (You'll discover many overlapping traits from each list.) The list below of 20 sociopathic traits is taken directly from the book *Without Conscience: The Disturbing World of the Psychopaths Among Us* by Dr. Robert D. Hare, Ph.D:

1. Glib and superficial charm. The tendency to be smooth, engaging, charming, slick, and verbally facile. Sociopathic charm is not in the least shy, self-conscious, or afraid to say anything. A sociopath never gets tongue-tied. They have freed themselves from the social conventions about taking turns in talking, for example.

2. Grandiose self-worth. A grossly inflated view of one's abilities and self-worth, self-assured, opinionated, cocky, a braggart. Sociopaths are arrogant people who believe they are superior human beings.

3. Need for stimulation or proneness to boredom. An excessive need for novel, thrilling, and exciting stimulation; taking chances and doing things that are risky. Sociopaths often have low self-discipline in carrying tasks through to completion because they get bored easily. They fail to work at the same job for any length of time, for example, or to finish tasks that they consider dull or routine.

4. Pathological lying. Can be moderate or high; in moderate form, they will be shrewd, crafty, cunning, sly, and clever; in extreme form, they will be deceptive, deceitful, underhanded, unscrupulous, manipulative, and dishonest.

5. Conning and manipulative. The use of deceit and deception to cheat, con, or defraud others for personal gain; distinguished from Item #4 in the degree to which exploitation and callous ruthlessness is present, as reflected in a lack of concern for the feelings and suffering of one's victims.

6. Lack of remorse or guilt. A lack of feelings or concern for the losses, pain, and suffering of victims; a tendency to be unconcerned, dispassionate, coldhearted, and unempathic. This item is usually demonstrated by a disdain for one's victims.

7. Shallow affect. Emotional poverty or a limited range or depth of feelings; interpersonal coldness in spite of signs of open gregariousness.

8. Callousness and lack of empathy. A lack of feelings toward people in general; cold, contemptuous, inconsiderate, and tactless.

9. Parasitic lifestyle. An intentional, manipulative, selfish, and exploitative financial dependence on others as reflected in a

       lack of motivation, low self-discipline, and inability to begin or complete responsibilities.

10. Poor behavioral controls. Expressions of irritability, annoyance, impatience, threats, aggression, and verbal abuse; inadequate control of anger and temper; acting hastily.

11. Promiscuous sexual behavior. A variety of brief, superficial relations, numerous affairs, and an indiscriminate selection of sexual partners; the maintenance of several relationships at the same time; a history of attempts to sexually coerce others into sexual activity or taking great pride at discussing sexual exploits or conquests.

12. Early behavior problems. A variety of behaviors prior to age 13, including lying, theft, cheating, vandalism, bullying, sexual activity, fire-setting, glue-sniffing, alcohol use, and running away from home.

13. Lack of realistic, long-term goals. An inability or persistent failure to develop and execute long-term plans and goals; a nomadic existence, aimless, lacking direction in life.

14. Impulsivity. The occurrence of behaviors that are unpremeditated and lack reflection or planning; inability to resist temptation, frustrations, and urges; a lack of deliberation without considering the consequences; foolhardy, rash, unpredictable, erratic, and reckless.

15. Irresponsibility. Repeated failure to fulfill or honor obligations and commitments; such as not paying bills, defaulting on loans, performing sloppy work, being absent or late to work, failing to honor contractual agreements.

16. Failure to accept responsibility for own actions. A failure to accept responsibility for one's actions reflected in low conscientiousness, an absence of dutifulness, antagonistic manipulation, denial of responsibility, and an effort to manipulate others through this denial.

17. Many short-term marital relationships. A lack of commitment to a long-term relationship reflected in inconsistent, undependable, and unreliable commitments in life, including marital.

18. Juvenile delinquency. Behavior problems between the ages of 13-18; mostly behaviors that are crimes or clearly involve aspects of antagonism, exploitation, aggression, manipulation, or a callous, ruthless tough-mindedness.

19. Revocation of condition release. A revocation of probation or other conditional release due to technical violations, such as carelessness, low deliberation, or failing to appear.

20. Criminal versatility. A diversity of types of criminal offenses, regardless if the person has been arrested or convicted for them; taking great pride at getting away with crimes (Hare 2011).

In addition to the above two lists of traits, the biggest trait (or magic trick, as I like to call it) that makes narcissistic sociopaths so dangerous and effective is their ability to go unnoticed by the rest of us. They can do this, because they are good at pretending (lying) and wearing many masks (again, lying). Simply put, they lie to themselves and everyone else. They lie so much that some of them are convinced of their own lies, which is where evil is born.

Story Introduction

This is the story of a seemingly innocent little boy who grows into a ferocious, conscienceless, ugly monster that destroys and devours everything good and pure that crosses his path. From tender childhood friendships to sweet innocent romances, nothing is immune to the monster's dark spell and insidious nature.

This is also a story of survival and hope: survival of intimate partner abuse and hope that one day there will be an end to domestic violence and to the suffering of the silent victims.

Part 1

Behold, a Son

It started innocently enough. Like most births, he arrived between the legs of his mother. (A plain woman, most who knew her would claim.) His father held him for a moment and proclaimed, "Behold, a son!" That was about the extent of the fanfare, for this was his father's second child, second son. Plus, the old man never really had much to say anyhow. So, the mother, who was much younger than the old man, tended dutifully to the needs of her boys while the old man busied himself with his business.

Part 2

Growing Years to Age 10

The boy and his family lived simply. The old man worked; the mother worked. They lived in a modest home in the ghetto of the Capital City. The boy and his brother played and battled. But the boy seemed to be the "favorite" and was always given exactly what he asked for and demanded. The mother rarely said no to the boy. But his brother often received little comfort and attention. If the boy felt slighted, he went into temper tantrum rages until his way was heeded. The mother was at a loss about how to handle the boy. (She failed to realize that her mothering skills were the problem. But she just didn't want her handsome little boy subjected to the ugliness she endured as a child.) So, instead of setting boundaries and modeling love and care for the boy, the mother continued to coddle her baby boy, often ignoring the brother who grew to despise her. (After all, the brother was just a replica of the old man, in her eyes. There wasn't much cute or endearing about the brother. But that is an entirely different tale. Let's get back to the monster, shall we?)

Once the boy reached school age, he was enrolled in a private school. Even though the public schools in the ghettos of the Capital City outperformed the majority of schools across the Land, the mother insisted on a private education. (After all, she came from a Far Land where public schools sucked.) Thanks to the mother's doting, the boy felt more and more entitled and special. He viewed himself as the exception to the other poor ghetto boys, whom he considered lowly and dull. He was far superior to any of them! (At least as far as his twisted little mind was concerned.)

Part 3

The Move to the Far Land

The mother and old man saved many pennies from working and running the old man's business. They decided to move to the Far Land, where luxuries were much cheaper than in the Capital City. So, when the boy was about 11, he moved from the ghetto to the heart of the beautiful Resort City by the ocean in the Far Land.

Here his sense of entitlement and ego grew even bigger. The boy attended private schools, played sports in private clubs, lived in large homes. The mother and old man did not work. Instead, they built homes, spent money on vacations, gorged themselves on food, and sunned themselves like lizards, day in and day out, along the sea. They became fat and lazy and concerned themselves less and less with the boy and his brother.

But the boy didn't seem to mind their absence. He loved his independence and eventually, after his brother left to return to the Capital City, learned how to cook and clean and make his own money and do his own laundry. These skills were all he needed, he thought. He didn't need anyone else to survive. Life was easy and carefree. He was on the verge of discovering the world.

Yet, who could ever imagine that so much independence, that being left alone at such a young age, would destroy the boy's understanding of love, empathy, and grief? Could the boy ever find those three things that he was clearly missing? Did he even understand that they were missing in the first place?

Part 4

El Conquistador o El Destructor?

The boy had a lovely childhood friend who adored him. She shared her secrets and dreams of becoming an architect. She taught him about the history of the beautiful buildings and homes scattered throughout the Resort City. She was so enthusiastic when they were together. In her innocence, she never questioned his commitment. She interpreted their love of so many similar things and ideas as the stuff of "soul mates." She had no idea that he viewed her as nothing more than a tool, something that would help him improve himself. Over time, he successfully sucked her energy dry, taking advantage of her of her sweetness and abusing her vulnerabilities. But before tossing her aside, he screwed her, finally exhausting her usefulness to him. Then he walked away, never to look back. To the boy she became "La Chica Loca" from the Far Land. She was devastated and left feeling as cold and empty as a once beautiful building, abandoned to slowly decay and grow ugly with the slow passing of time.

As each year and each woman passed through his life, the boy became accomplished at sucking and tossing aside souls. By the time he was 25 years old, he had left the broken hearts of nearly 100 women in his wake. (And to think that, legally, a person becomes an adult at 18. Not true in the case of the boy.) No love lost for him.

It seemed there would be no love until he met "The French Girl." Aaaaah! Just listening to him say her name would make one think he loved her. But no, he didn't love her either. He loved the idea of her. He loved how impressed others would be to learn his girlfriend was from Paris (even though she was actually from Toulouse, about 8 hours south of Paris!) He also thought he'd learn French and get lots of free trips to France out of the deal. Wow! He WAS in love! (What a loser . . ."The French Girl," that is.)

Soon, he grew tired of "The French Girl." For one thing, she spoke too much French. (Duh!) And for another, she hadn't offered a single trip. (The gull! Oh, shit, I mean, gall!) Besides, the boy thought she was so, so boring and depressed all of the time. (How could he be expected to put up with that?) So, he cheated on her with some women from the local bar. No skin off his back. The relationship had run its course, according to his calculations. So what if they were still living together. Right? He was right, right? (Dead wrong, douche bag!)

By the time the boy reached 30, he was still not married or with children. He often thought to himself, "If my fat pig of an older brother can land a wife and conceive a child, why the hell can't I? After all, I am the better-looking one. People tell me all the time that I got all of the good genes and my brother got the dregs." So, the way most people go in search of a new house or car, the boy went in search of a wife.

Part 5

Practice Makes Perfect

The boy didn't really know where to begin his journey to find the perfect wife. So, he decided to do a practice run. (Practice run? Yeah, you know, like a test drive but with a wife, not a car. Ethical, huh?) The boy concluded that this approach would yield the best ROI (for my more evolved readers, that's business speak for return on investment).

So, the boy took a short vacation from the Capital City's hustle and bustle and visited the remote childhood home of his father in the Far Land. Within hours of arriving, he reconnected with his much younger and inexperienced cousin. He immediately sensed her desperation and desire to experience something beyond the village where she was born and raised. He said to himself, "She will make the perfect practice wife. She's not beautiful, but she'll do."

During their short courtship, he promised her love, tenderness, opportunity, and adventure. (All lies.) She adored him and quickly became enamored. To her, the boy, her cousin, represented success and strength, qualities that the majority of men in her Far Land village lacked. When the boy proposed marriage (just a few weeks after reconnecting), the cousin did not hesitate to say yes. Soon, he had a wife, a wedding portrait, and a growing business (his father's old business, not a business the boy worked to establish for himself. Are you kidding!? That would have been *waaay* too much work).

Part 6

List of Criteria for an Acceptable Wife

The boy realized within a few weeks of living with his cousin, his wife, that she was definitely NOT the kind of wife he wanted. Although she was quiet and always agreeable, she was boring. She lacked a formal education beyond the high school level (so did the boy but HIS credentials could always be masked, or so he thought), she failed to turn him on sexually, she had a bad profile and ugly teeth, and she simply had nothing to offer him that he could use to improve his reputation or standing in the community or with his friends (of which he had few).

So, instead of fostering a relationship of care and love, the boy decided to live like he was single. He ignored his wife and often ate before arriving home. (His parents had squandered all of the pennies they had saved and were forced to move back to the Capital City to work again. They lived around the corner from the boy. Still considering the boy her beloved favorite, the mother prepared him evening meals every day. He'd stop there on his way home, never thinking to invite his wife along.) The boy also enjoyed playing basketball and soccer and chose to practice EVERY spare moment he had, further alienating his wife from his life.

The boy had many sordid affairs while married to his cousin. He was amazed at the ease of bedding women even as a married man. He used this opportunity to fine-tune his list of criteria for the perfect wife. Before, when he was younger, the boy hadn't paid much attention to the possible good qualities of women beyond their attractiveness. (Women are only good for sex, right?) He soon realized that he needed a woman who was smart and educated (but not too smart), who had a wealthy family, who had skills and resources he did not possess, and who was in desperate need to get married and have babies immediately.

He soon learned (through astute observation) that women approaching 30 or in their early thirties were the most vulnerable and easily swayed by charm and romance. (Oh, and he had THAT mastered!)

But wait; we're getting ahead of ourselves. What's he going to do with his practice wife? How is he going to make getting a divorce look like something that was HER idea? He sought advice from, who else, his wily mother, who told him, "Whatever you do, don't get her pregnant." (Oh! That's brilliant advice, don't you think?) If you want to be able to dump someone on the side of the road and never look back, make sure you don't leave behind any evidence. A kid, a grandchild, would keep you forever connected to someone you want to toss in the garbage pile of life. (Yeah, don't get her pregnant. Jesus!)

The boy lucked out. His wife, his cousin, sensed he was unhappy, and as any obedient, codependent sidekick would do, she gave him a quick divorce. Soon he was back on the prowl for that perfect wife . . .

Wait. Wait. Wait! I keep getting ahead of myself . . .

Waaaay back when the boy and his cousin were just courting, the boy had planned a trip for two to Paris (one of his ploys to make his cousin swoon at his romantic nature). Just a few weeks before the divorce was to be final, they took that *cough* trip *cough* for two *cough* to Paris. Only, there was ABSOLUTELY NOTHING romantic about it.

Part 7

Pre-Divorce Paris Trip

Upon boarding the flight to Paris, the boy was offered a seat in first class at a huge discount. (But there was only one seat. He wouldn't . . . he couldn't . . . he didn't? Oh, yes, he would, could, AND did!) While his wife, his cousin, sat squeezed between two strangers for the six-hour flight across the Atlantic, the boy sat comfortably in first class listening to music and wearing a sleep mask for the duration (insert any picture of a douche bag here). Not a worry in his mind. He was on his way to see his idol.

Idol, you ask? Yes. Even though the boy had little respect or empathy for the real people in his life, he had an overwhelming admiration *foooor* . . . guess who . . . Jim Morrison!!!! You're shaking your head, right? Jim Morrison was a drug-addicted rock star who abused women, alcohol, sex, and life in general. Who could idolize such a creep? The boy, that's who! The boy even thought he resembled the dead poet. (Yeah, maybe when the boy is six feet under with worms coming out of his mouth!)

Once in Paris and safely registered in his hotel room (which he shared with his wife, his cousin, who slept on the sofa while he slept under the 1000-thread count sheets on the bed), the boy meticulously unpacked his clothes and laid out his perfume (do NOT call it cologne, OK?) and other toiletries in the wash room. He then set out for JM's grave.

You're probably wondering where the cousin, his wife, was while the boy explored Paris, right? She walked dutifully behind him along the avenues and streets and through the winding metro stairwells. The boy (the piece of garbage) simply ignored her. In his mind, she was dead to him. She served him no further purpose other than burdening him with her loneliness on this trip. Plus, he was doing her a favor by ALLOWING her to see the world alongside him, right? After all, he is an exceptional human being with an enormous intellect (but rather a small and unfortunate penis) and huge heart. (*Riiiiight!* a heart made of TNT, perhaps!)

After getting stuffed with crepes and pricked by roses placed on JM's grave each of the five mornings he spent in Paris, the two returned home. Back in the Capital City, the divorce went through and the boy no longer had a wife! He was FINALLY ready to continue his search for the perfect wife.

Part 8
Stuff the Boy Will NEVER Understand

For all of the searching the boy did, he could never find the perfect woman he so desperately wanted and NEEDED. (You see, he NEEDED a woman to feel powerful and in control. His Pomeranian wouldn't live as long as a woman could. He NEEDED a woman!) He often asked himself, "Why don't these women listen and just do what I want them to do (like a dog)? Why can't they just love me the way I want to be loved (like a dog does)? Why do they treat me so badly when all I do for them is love them (like a dog)?" Let's try to answer these deep questions for the sociopath, shall we?

Women are not dogs. ~ Dogs have zero opinions and can't talk back to you. They just lick you for food and let you know when they need to do their business. A dog is NOT capable of a mutual relationship.

Women are humans. ~ Humans have individual brains, emotions, and feelings that are legitimate and real. When a sociopath (like the boy) continues to disregard the value of her individuality, she will NEVER love him the way he wants her to love him because love starts with respect, and he, the boy, doesn't respect her.

Women are smart. ~ When a sick and twisted sociopath (like the boy) uses flattery and charm and manipulation to get what he wants (sex, money, food, a good deal on a new car . . .), a woman with any kind of backbone and intelligence will soon see through his ruse. She will begin to ask herself, "Why did I fall in love with this horrible and uncaring man? Is he going to treat me like shit, too? Is he going to talk about me like this when we break up? Is he going to tell everyone that I'm crazy, too? (Yes, yes, and yes.)

Women don't NEED you. ~ Women love to be loved. But women do not NEED a man (the boy especially) to get them through their day and to be happy. Women have many, many things going on inside of their minds that keep them busy and engaged in life. (Besides, the only thing the boy has that women don't have is a penis, and his is a shameful and diseased one at that.)

You're probably asking, "If this guy is such a narcissistic sociopath, how was he able to get married, divorced, and engaged 3 times in 5 years? What kind of woman would be attracted to him?"

Part 9

What Kind of Crazy Person Would Date a Sociopath?

Normal, non-sociopathic people desire to love and be loved. Sociopaths, like the boy, take advantage of this human characteristic and target anyone who is willing to invite them into their lives (like vampires).

In the honeymoon phase of new relationships, the boy (all sociopaths, for that matter) showers his victims with gifts and praises and promises of a beautiful life together. The boy's favorite lines are, "You are the love of my life. You are the One I want to grow old with. I could NEVER make love to anyone else ever again. If you leave me, I'll die." Who wouldn't melt having this whispered into her ear or repeatedly texted to her throughout their day? A fantasy is created. The victim falls fast. She doesn't even know what hit her.

Then the praises and promises become less frequent and the criticism begins (within a matter of months). The boy claims that she doesn't kiss him correctly or long enough. She doesn't call enough. (These "mini pity parties" make the boy seem insecure, so the woman does everything to reassure the boy she loves him). She cooks for him, walks his dog, folds his laundry, makes love to him every time he asks.

Yet, it's still not good enough. He starts to comment about her hair and her clothes and suggests she try this or that (knowing she will resist).

And she does resist because THOSE clothes or fashions don't fit who she is. The boy becomes enraged. The woman caves and starts dressing in what makes him happy.

But he is STILL not happy. Now he begins criticizing her career and insists she should look for something different, "Babe, you could do better. Those people don't appreciate you. I would quit if I were you. You need a job closer to me. Wouldn't it be nice to have lunch together every day?" So, she actively begins looking for a new job thinking he'll be supportive and willing to help her with the process. Instead, he insists it's taking her too long and that she must not be trying very hard to find something else and that, if she really cared to spend more time with him, she'd have a new job by now.

Finally, at this stage, the woman begins feeling like something is not quite right. "Why can't he see that I am trying? Why can't he see that I do care and love him? Why is what I do never good enough?" But these worries are fleeting, because the boy quickly distracts her by surprising her with a gift: "It's a journal I found at your favorite store. You should start writing that book you always talk about writing?" How sweet, she thinks. He does know I love and care for him and he loves and cares for me.

A few days later, the woman is writing in her new journal. She sees the boy pacing through the hall and asks, "Why are you pacing?" He explains, "Why aren't you out here hanging out with me or talking to me about my day?" Quizzically, she responds, "Well, we just had dinner together and talked about our days, and now I'm relaxing and writing for a bit. What in the world is wrong with you?!?" (Oh, shit! The woman has vocalized her internal worries that have been driving her crazy. NOT. WHAT. THE. BOY. CAN. HANDLE.)

The rage ensues. The boy screams, "You treat me like shit! You don't appreciate anything I do for you. You push me away. You don't love me. I NEED you to NEED me!"

The woman is dumbfounded and wonders to herself, "What have I done to make him feel this way? How can I make him feel more loved?" She apologizes, puts down her journal, and follows him to the sofa where they watch a movie.

After the movie, the woman thinks about calling her mom or sister just to chat about her feelings and be reassured that everything will be fine. (Besides, all couples have arguments, right?) She reaches for her phone and sees the boy watching her out of the corner of his eye. Suddenly, a feeling of anxiety rushes through her. "He is going to view me calling my family as a betrayal," she realizes. She doesn't want to upset him knowingly, so she puts the phone down and reaches for another glass of wine. (Is this what walking-on-eggshells feels like? Hmmm? I think so!)

The next morning while driving to work, the woman calls her mother. Instead of receiving reassurance, the woman hears, "What is wrong with you? What happened to your backbone? Why are you letting the boy control you like this? Don't you see how jealous and manipulative he is? YOU have done nothing but accommodate his every whim."

The woman thinks about her mother's words and makes a mental list of what she has done for the boy, from changing jobs to changing the way she holds her fork. (That's a bit of an exaggeration but you get the point, right?) She glances at herself in the rearview mirror and doesn't recognize the reflection. "Who is this tired, hung-over, depressed woman looking back at me?" she asks herself. "Where did I go?"

That evening, the boy and the woman have a discussion over dinner about a friend of the boy. It seems the friend has been secretive about certain things in his life and the boy is livid about it. (Let's follow along with the discussion . . .)

Boy: "So, I wrote him an email today telling him that he is dead to me."

Woman: "What? He has been your best friend for years. How can you just write him off in an email? Don't you want to hear his side?"

Boy: "His side? He lied to me."

Woman: "He kept something private from you. He didn't lie. There is a HUGE difference."

Boy: "What are you saying . . . that I am wrong for being upset? You really don't like me, do you? You just LOOK for reasons to hate me."

Woman: "Seriously? I hate that you would tell someone who was such a huge part of your life that he is dead to you now. He doesn't owe you anything. He had his reasons and you need to deal with it. Or are you lying to me about why you are no longer friends?"

Boy: "Why don't you just get the FUCK out of MY house NOW!?!?!"

(Do you recognize the pattern leading to his rages, yet? No? Don't worry; there are more examples to come. I promise.)

The woman held her glass of wine not knowing how the heck to respond. (After all, the boy had been begging her for months to move in with him, expressing how he wanted his house to be "Our home.")

The woman stood frozen and just stared at the boy as he raged. The boy's entire being became distorted. His teeth transformed into fangs and his shoulders became more and more rounded and curled forward ready to attack. The monster revealed itself, and it was hideous!

In her trance, the woman could not hear what the boy was saying or comprehend where she was until she found herself outside with no shoes, no coat, no phone, no purse, no keys, and no understanding of what the hell just happened. (Wake up, Lady! This guy is a nut job!)

She sat on the front steps. What was she going to do now? Who was going to help her? She had successfully ignored all of the warnings her friends and family gave her about the boy. They said many times that he was not good for her, that he was too possessive, jealous, and selfish. But the woman chose to ignore them, hoping the boy REALLY was a good person.

The woman decided she would start walking. She could think. But then she realized she had no shoes. She was angry. "What the hell is he thinking just throwing me out like this?" she thought. So, she started pounding on the door. The dog barked from behind the door. There was no other sound. She kept knocking . . . and knocking . . . and knocking. Her anger turned into frustration. Her frustration turned into sadness. She sat on the steps again, leaned against the railing, and simply cried until she exhausted herself and fell to sleep.

She awoke many hours later in her bed, in their bed. Gentle music was coming from the next room. The aroma of something delicious filled the air. She looked at the clock; it was nearly midnight.

"What is going on? I don't remember going to bed."

The boy stepped into the room. The look on his face was one of concern. "How are you feeling, Baby? You scared me," said the boy.

"Huh?" the woman thought to herself. "How did I get here?" she said aloud.

"You rolled down the front steps and got knocked unconscious. You don't remember do you?"

The woman started to speak excitedly about how she remembers knocking on the door, and he didn't answer and . . . but her head started to pound, and she couldn't concentrate on her words through the pain.

The boy was now leaning over her with a glass of water, caressing her back and saying, "Take a sip. You need to relax. Dinner is almost ready. I made your favorite." He smiled impudently above her.

(Can you believe the boy? He got away with it! Poor Lady.)

Part 10
Ghosts

The boy loved pictures and photographs, specifically photographs of himself looking smart. (You know, intelligent AND well-dressed.) He had framed images of himself EVERYWHERE in his home. Pictures of him with short hair, with long hair, in dress clothes, in uniforms . . . . His face was around every corner the woman ventured. The images told her nothing except that the boy must really love himself. The woman wanted to learn more about the boy, but whenever she would ask him about his past and his childhood, the boy was always hesitant, secretive, and unwilling to share.

One evening the boy left for a piano lesson. (Why piano? The boy secretly wished he had been born a rock star, but he lacked the voice and tried the guitar with no luck. So, he thought pounding keys would be easier. And, OF COURSE, he hoped to impress future women by learning to play "Clocks" by Cold Play. How ironic, huh? . . ."Come out upon my seas/Cursed missed opportunities/Am I a part of the cure/Or am I part of the disease?" That's an easy one to answer.)

While he was out, the woman searched and searched for other pictures or journals or anything that would reveal the boy for her. She couldn't find anything until she started snooping (I know, she shouldn't be doing that) in the storage room in the boy's basement. She hit the jackpot: photo albums from the boy's past!

She looked through page after page of albums. She smiled and laughed as she saw the boy grow up in the images. Unfortunately, as she moved through each consecutive album, she discovered more and more empty spaces where images had once been stored. Ghosts. Who were they, and why had they been removed?

The woman spent the evening thinking that the missing photos made no sense to her, at least not human and logical sense. Why would anyone remove pictures of specific people? Why would someone bother with such a tedious task? (The answer: because the boy is a sociopath and prefers to act like people from his past never existed, because they either challenged him or wore out their usefulness.)

As she attempts to understand, she remembers, when they first started dating, how jealous and angry he was to discover her old online blog containing references to her ex. He made her delete it, the entire blog; he insisted on it! (The woman wasn't completely deluded. She secretly saved the content in a hidden file on her computer. After all, it was her history, her memories. No one burns their journals, do they?)

So, she assumes all of the missing images were of his ex-wife, past fiancées, and girlfriends that he removed so SHE wouldn't get jealous. (That WOULD make sense if the albums weren't in storage, lady!!!)

And she couldn't help from wondering, "Will I become a ghost space in an album one day?"

(Of course you will!)

Part 11

First=Class Family Bonding?

The boy liked to think that he and his family had a very "evolved and mature relationship." When the woman asked why he never hugged his mother or told her he loved her, the boy explained, "My mother knows how I feel. She's just not that kind of mother." (Hmmmm? Strange that the boy didn't say, "I love my mother. Maybe I should hug her more." And what kind of mother doesn't want to receive love from her children?)

The boy later made a joke about the woman's concern.

The Boy: "Guess what I did today?"

The Woman: "What?!"

The Boy: "I hugged my mother! I told her that you said I don't show her enough affection. She just laughed."

The woman said nothing but thought to herself: "Uh, he thinks this is a joke! I think it's sick that he would hug her only after I mentioned something, and it's even more sick that he shared with her what I said."

Later that evening, the boy and the woman visited his mother and father for dinner. His brother and niece were also there. After dinner, his mother was playing with his niece and accidentally knocked the little girl off balance. The brother screamed at his mother, "You stupid fat cow!! Don't EVER touch my daughter like that again! You stupid fat cow!" The mother just cowered away. (Yeah, I am aware of the pun.)

The woman was speechless. She nudged the boy to do something about his brother's hateful behavior. (Who speaks to his mother with such disrespect?) The boy (who had an impish smirk on his face) just shrugged his shoulders as if there was nothing he could do. The father sat limp, as well. (Really? This is acceptable and evolved behavior?)

There would never be an apology from the brother, and there would never be a conversation with the brother letting him know his behavior was not acceptable. To the boy's family, the brother's disrespectful outburst was acceptable. The mother had been careless. (Hell. The niece wasn't even hurt!)

The woman was too afraid to start a conversation about it with the mother or the boy. She remained quiet and reached for another glass of wine and longed to be anywhere but there. (Do you see a pattern forming? Why doesn't she dump his ass already!!??!!)

Part 12

Judgment is Not Honesty

To the members of the boy's inner circle (which could be counted on one hand), he was a "stand-up" kind of guy. (Whatever that's supposed to mean, right?) His friends thought he was funny and witty and honest. (Honest? Really?) Yes, honest. The boy actually prided himself on his honesty. "If someone doesn't like what I have to say, I guess they simply can't handle the truth," he would say.

His favorite example of his honesty was when his sister-in-law (the wife of his "fat-pig-of-a brother") showed up at an evening event wearing something that the boy thought to be inappropriate ("at least for HER figure"). Upon seeing her, the boy's eyes immediately bulged, and he chuckled saying, "Wow, you look like a cream puff. Hahahaha!"

(Hmmmm? He must be confusing judgment with honesty. Not exactly the same things, are they?) He refused to apologize after the sister-in-law tried to explain that his comment was simply rude and that it hurt her feelings. "Pfft! She should have looked in the mirror before leaving the house," the boy countered.

The woman was also a recipient of the boy's "honesty." Daily, he would oscillate between flattery and downright disgust for some of the woman's choices in clothes. (I know. Petty, right? But it's these petty things that slowly erode a person's ability to like and love themselves over time.)

From things like, "Oh, wow! You wore that to work today? I wouldn't have been able to concentrate on work if I worked next to you." To more callous comments like, "Um, what were you thinking wearing THOSE shoes?" The woman never quite knew what to expect from his spewing mouth. Endearments or cattiness?

Over time, the woman simply stopped paying attention to any of his comments. She didn't know what to believe. Did he adore her or think she was a whore? Jesus! It was so difficult to know between his rages and then his apologies, both of which grew more common over time.

However, when it came to the boy's "honest" remarks about the woman's 5-year-old son (with her ex-husband), the woman had zero tolerance. What grown man can feel jealousy toward an innocent child and act on those jealousies through verbal and physical intimidation? The boy, that's who!!!

Part 13
This is Child Abuse

The boy COULD NOT handle sharing the woman's attention with her son. The boy NEEDED her to be focused on him at all times. (Otherwise, the woman would actually have something going on outside of the boy. He couldn't handle that. She needed to need him, he thought. And what better way of doing that than by injecting himself into every situation involving the child.)

The woman's son loved the boy's dog and played with him from the moment he awoke in the morning until he fell asleep at night. The dog was small enough not to hurt the child, and the child was gentle enough not to hurt the dog. (At least that's how any normal person would have viewed their interactions. But remember, the boy isn't normal, is he?)

The boy insisted that the child not "do this" and not "do that" to HIS dog. The woman attempted to reassure the boy that her son was gentle, and if her son did anything to hurt the dog, SHE (not the boy) would discipline the child. (Something out of the boy's control? Oh, the boy can't have that, can he?) He just ignored the woman's request and spoke to the child as he pleased.

As you can imagine, the child was often in tears (tears of frustration and confusion) because he never, ever hurt the dog, but the boy insisted that he WAS hurting the dog. (Imagine being 5 and asked not to do something. You don't do it, but you keep getting accused of doing it. This is emotional abuse. This is what destroys a child's ability to understand boundaries and consequences. THIS IS CHILD ABUSE! If you don't think so, ask your psychiatrist or get one for yourself, you probably need it.)

And that is just one example of the boy's abuse of the child. Here are several more:

The child was VERY choosy about what he ate (much like the boy was). However, the boy refused to allow the child to eat what he liked and often forced him to eat certain foods he KNEW the boy hated. This was nearly EVERY meal the child shared with the woman (his mother) and the boy. What did the woman do? She pleaded with the boy to allow the child to eat what he wanted. It was hard enough to get him to eat enough of the things he did like; it was impossible to get him to eat what he didn't. The boy ignored the woman's concerns. The child often sat alone at the table crying at his plate, BEGGING for "his mommy" to let him up. But if she let him up, the boy would go into a rage (yes, in front of the child) and scream, "How can you undermine me in front of him!!??!!" (What an asshole, huh?)

The boy always wanted to be empowered to tell the child when and for how long to take a bath. The woman would stand in the hall outside the closed bathroom door, listening to her son cry. "What the hell is the boy doing to my child? My child loves baths. He's going to ruin it for him." What was the boy doing? He was washing the child instead of allowing the child to play and wash himself. He also used water that was too hot on his tender scalp to rinse out the shampoo. Cruel and torturous. But the boy always denied he was doing anything wrong. It got to the point that the woman would not allow the bathroom door to be shut when her son bathed. And that SHE would bathe him. The boy was still able to find power and control in telling her she didn't clean him well enough or scrub him long enough. (The boy is crazy! Why couldn't he just let it go? Let her be the mother, the parent. Who was he but a burden and abuser in the child's life? And in the woman's life too.)

The boy talked "baby talk" to the child. (Talking baby talk isn't good when talking to infants, let alone 5-year-old boys. Even if you don't have children, you figure that out quickly, don't you?) The child hated the baby talk and would ask the boy to stop. The boy would never stop. The boy also liked to call the child a "midget" IN baby talk. The child would scream for him to stop calling him that, and the woman asked him not to call the child such a demeaning name. The boy just ignored them both and referred to the child however he desired.

The child felt like his desires didn't matter, that he didn't matter. Everything he did or said around the boy would be met with opposition. The boy even teased the child and called him a baby for hugging and kissing the woman so often. (Shouldn't he be encouraging the child to hug and kiss the woman? Oh, yeah, that's right! The boy doesn't hug and kiss HIS mother. Why would he encourage something as silly as hugging and kissing?) The child always felt unwanted and hurt around the boy. The child often told the woman, his mother, that he HATED the boy. The mother said, "You don't hate anyone, sweetheart. The boy will eventually understand and stop doing it."

(At least that is what she hoped. After all, the boy said she was the love of his life, his soul mate, the One, so he should feel genuine love for her child one day, right? Wishing and hoping do not bear much fruit when dealing with the abusive boy. He doesn't understand what love is. Hasn't the woman figured that out, yet?!?!?)

Part 14

I Want to be Adored!

The more the boy raged and apologized and raged and apologized, the less the woman wanted to express herself or her love. She began to retreat. (And this is only after a few months of feeling like her life was a fairy tale and that her Prince Charming had finally entered her life. She even had a 2-carat diamond ring that lost its sparkle under her gaze. It meant nothing to her if there was no harmony.) She went to work, ate, and slept. (She also drank more and more wine each night just so she could pass out early and not deal with the boy's smarmy remarks and silent treatment. It was hell on earth, she often thought. But she was powerless to escape; at least that's what she thought.)

Instead of trying to understand the woman and her obvious depressed state (which is what people in love do, right?), the boy only noticed what he wasn't getting from the woman: attention and adoration! For the boy, this monster sociopath, relationships are all about him, "What's in this for me? Sex, money, power, admiration?" It could be anything, just as long as it is something that makes the boy SEEM better in the eyes of others and make people want to be him. (This is really sick and twisted thinking.)

So, when the boy felt neglected by the woman, he sought the attention of other women. (Brilliant solution, don't you think? That's what ALL men in love do, don't you know?) And there were MANY other women:

Remember the French Girl? The boy never really let her go, because she provided him with lots and lots of needed attention. It didn't matter that she was married with children and lived 250 miles away. (The distance actually benefited the boy; easier to avoid messiness that way, huh?) The boy wrote letters to the French Girl whenever the woman seemed distant. He always complained about the woman and said she didn't love him like he loved her or appreciate everything he did for her. The French Girl responded with reassurance that the boy was worthy of love and deserved better than the woman. (Maybe the French Girl was better? Who knows?) Oh, and the boy would send her pictures of himself (again looking "smart"), and the French Girl would return the favor with pictures of herself. (Aaaahhhh! Ain't love grand?)

He also had "La Chica Loco" (his friend from the Far Land who taught him to appreciate architecture, remember?) in his back pocket. La Chica showered the boy with nourishment for his ego. She often wrote to or phoned him, begging him to leave the woman and move to the Far Land and marry her and have children together. She BEGGED. But the boy didn't love La Chica. He was "repulsed" by her. (Repulsed, yes, the boy's word!) The boy allowed La Chica to think he loved her too, knowing he had zero interest or intentions of EVER being with her. (How cruel!! If La Chica only knew what a monster he had become. No one loves monsters, do they?)

So, the boy would get his ego stroked just as often as needed and continued to believe that the woman didn't love him. (At least not the way he wanted the woman to love him.) The boy didn't realize that the woman DID love him, unconditionally, she simply didn't agree with EVERYTHING he said or did. And the boy was extremely bad at communicating when there was any kind of opposition to his way of thinking. (Uuuggghh! Just get over yourself and learn how to embrace someone else's opinion. It doesn't mean you have to agree every single time, but the other person deserves respect, not just your rage. Wow!)

Part 15

"It's Not Me; It's You!"

The boy was desperate to marry the woman and have children. He NEEDED that license and certificate and the woman to take his name. It was another possession to him. He wanted to possess the woman and eventually any children they bore. But, as you can suspect, the woman's doubts about a happy future with the boy grew each day.

Not only did he abuse the woman with words and rage in the privacy of his home, the boy soon began to publicly humiliate the woman. He enjoyed the walk-away-and-give-her-the-silent-treatment act. This was EVERYWHERE! Walking in the park, shopping in the mall, strolling along busy city sidewalks. And the woman would follow behind him begging for him to talk to her, "Just tell me what I did? Tell me why you are just ignoring me?" He said nothing and just kept walking ahead. The boy could keep this up for hours, leaving the woman worn and doubting herself. "I must have really upset him somehow, but how? What is wrong with me? Why am I hurting him like this?" (Wake up, Lady! You are not hurting the boy; he's damaged beyond repair and trying to damage you, too.)

The boy loved seeing her beg. He enjoyed knowing he had so much control over her happiness. Yet, he often wondered why she was so depressed and drinking more and more. (To escape your crazy making, c%$# sucker!) He kept blaming her family for not intervening. "Your family just lets you do whatever you want to do because they are afraid to stand up to you. They are blind to the fact that you are hurting yourself and will eventually die if something isn't done." He tried convincing her that she had a serious drinking problem and suffered from bipolar disorder. The woman became more and more convinced that he could be right. After all, why would the boy treat her the way he treated her unless she deserved to be treated that way? (Do you sense the insidious nature of the boy's ability to mentally manipulate the woman? Good people are vulnerable to this type of emotional abuse. Even smart, educated people.)

And then they were pregnant . . .

Part 16

Property Rights

Before getting into the boy's feelings and approach to the woman's pregnancy, let's review the reasons why having a child with the boy is a REALLY bad idea. (More like, a tragic disaster!)

The boy considered the woman his property. There are many things he forbid his property from doing:

The woman was forbidden to freely pursue friendships outside of the boy. Personal e-mails and phone calls were frowned upon. They took away from the attention the boy thought he deserved. Besides, the boy believes a friendship is only valuable if there is something "in it" for you. For example, the woman had a friend who had recently lost his wife and child. She reached out to her friend to support him and keep him from dwelling too much on his loss. The boy viewed this as fruitless, "Why do you talk to him? He is obviously unable to offer you ANYTHING. He probably just wants to fuck you or something. You're such a whore." The woman tried and tried but failed to convince the boy that her old friend just really needed someone to talk to about his loss; her old friend was clearly distraught and just needed a sympathetic ear and a shoulder to lean on. But her efforts were "fruitless." (Why could she not convince the boy? Because he has no heart and is unable to empathize with ANYONE!)

The woman was not permitted to use her computer in such a manner that would seem sneaky or suspicious to the boy. Activities like writing e-mails, commenting to posts by friends on social networks, shopping online, and/or surfing for nothing in particular were all threatening to the boy. If the boy couldn't see or investigate and approve her activity, then she MUST be doing something she wasn't supposed to be doing. And if he suspected she was doing any of these things, he would go into rage in order to find out. Just look what happened when the woman added password protection to her laptop so the boy couldn't snoop and invade her privacy:

Looks like a Macbook that's been bent over someone's knee, doesn't it? (Because it IS a laptop that has been bent over someone's knee! Can we say "sociopath" any louder?)

The woman was also forbidden to enter her ex-husband's home when picking up her son for the weekends. (Hmmmm? This makes zero sense considering life with a child is often unpredictable, and the woman enjoyed when her son wanted to show her something in his room at his father's home.) The woman often had to lie or keep certain secrets, which she hated. The boy would not budge on his orders.

The woman must come home directly from work each day. (No stopping on Go to collect $200.)

The woman was forbidden to write anything creative that doesn't mention or allude to the boy and was often criticized about her style and choice of words. (As if he had some kind of authority over the English language. He didn't even know the difference between connotation and denotation.) Therefore, the woman eventually stopped writing creatively altogether. (I wonder what the boy thinks of this story, completely dedicated to him? He must be so, so honored! But wait, this is just fiction, right?)

The woman was only allowed to wash clothes on certain days of the week. (It can't be explained, my dedicated readers, it cannot be explained.) Out of shear frustration, she stopped doing laundry also.

When the woman walked the boy's dog, she was ordered to walk a certain route. (You have GOT to be kidding!?) According to the boy, his dog would not "go" unless the dog walked THAT route. (Hmmmm? Makes no sense. If you gotta go, you're gonna go, right?)

If the woman finished her meal before the boy, at home or especially in a restaurant, the boy demanded that she wait until he finished his meal before she was allowed to have any coffee or dessert. And the boy was notorious for sending his food back to the kitchen because he was such a picky eater. (If there was something in the dish that he wouldn't eat, it was ALWAYS the waitress's fault, not his, for neglecting to read the menu more closely.) Sometimes, because of this, the woman would wait, and wait, and wait. (Jesus! Who would bother to be so patient with such a douche bag?)

As a direct effect of these crazy demands, the woman lost her ability to make her own choices. She was basically rendered dependent on the boy for direction and answers. (That's if she wanted to avoid his rages, which she dreaded more than anything she had ever experienced.)

By the time she discovered she was pregnant with the monster's child, she was lost, defenseless, and extremely emotionally vulnerable. Her spark had been extinguished. Her hope was lost.

Part 17

Pregnant

The woman knew her body and knew, even before taking a test, that she was pregnant. So many doubts filled her thoughts and caused great anxiety. On one hand, she feared telling the boy because she knew it was something he desperately wanted. "If I tell him, things will change and probably for the worse." She feared he would demand that she quit her job. She also worried that the boy would become more abusive of her child just because he had his own offspring on the way and didn't need to continue pretending he loved her child. (If you can call his behavior love.)

A few weeks went by. The woman was having severe nausea and knew she couldn't keep her secret much longer. She took another pregnancy test, placed it next to the boy (who was practicing that Cold Play song on the keyboard), and walked back to the bedroom before he could react.

She sat silently and anxiously on the bed. She heard the boy sigh, press off the power switch to the keyboard, push the bench away from the console, and stand to walk in her direction. The boy entered the room holding the test out in front of him, wagging it at the woman.

The Boy: "THIS is how you tell me? What is wrong with you?"

The Woman: "How did you want me to tell you? Should I scream for joy, wrap my arms around you, and pull out the baby magazines? I am not happy about this right now. I am sick or haven't you noticed?"

The Boy: "Just so you know, my mom will buy the furniture."

The woman didn't know what to think. Who cares who buys anything! The woman just wants to be happy. Having a baby should be a happy event. (At least that's how she felt when she was pregnant with her child years before.)

Instead of trying to battle the boy, the woman laid her head on her pillow in an attempt to control the overwhelming nausea washing over her. But the boy wanted to talk about this. The boy didn't care that she was feeling sick.

The Boy: "How can you sleep at a moment like this? I want to talk about things. You will NOT be picking up your son anymore. His father can bring him here and pick him up."

The Woman: "Are you serious? That's insane. His father and I share that responsibility. I WANT to pick up my son."

The Boy: "You won't while you're pregnant with MY child!"

Oh, Dear GOD! The woman wanted to run to the toilet and just puke. On top of the nausea, she had to deal with this asshole's unreasonable demands. Why did it matter? Why was wielding such control so important to the boy?

The woman prayed for a miscarriage. She couldn't bring a child into the world knowing this monster would be influencing it and molding it into . . . into a monster, too. She cried and slept.

Part 18
Shame & Hope

The boy let everyone know the good news about the pregnancy: his mother, his father, his brother, and his friend. (Yes, that was EVERYONE.) The woman, on the other hand, was too ashamed to tell anyone. She didn't even tell her mother or closest sister. She didn't want them to worry more than they already worried. After all, they witnessed the woman deteriorate from being vivacious and opinionated to becoming frightened and depressed in a very short period of time. Where was the woman they all remembered?

While the boy happily bounced around planning a nursery and shopping for baby things, the woman focused on taking care of herself and her son; thinking too much about what was to come only caused her nightmares and stress. She surrendered all decorating ideas and decisions to the boy. She was too weakened to fight a losing battle (many losing battles) and often wondered if it was too late to escape. (It's never too late, Lady, never too late!)

Then it happened. The woman suffered a miscarriage at 15 weeks. Luckily, she was home alone when it happened. She burst into tears of joy, even through the pain. From this point, the woman began planning her return to equilibrium. She did not tell the boy about the miscarriage; knowing the boy, he would accuse her of purposely harming herself to end the pregnancy. (Of course she hadn't hurt herself, but she couldn't help but think that her prayers had been answered. A second chance at a happy life.)

Part 19

The Escape Plan

The boy continued bringing home gifts for the baby. He'd present things like bibs and blankets and stuffed animals and toys. The woman had to feign excitement or the boy would question her love for him. When she asked him to slow down his shopping sprees, he accused her of caring more about her child with her ex-husband than the unborn child with him. (If only he knew how she REALLY felt.) The woman was simply exhausted from all the accusations and mental manipulations. She was more determined than ever to break free.

She planned to leave on the eve of her birthday and never look back. She viewed it as a symbolic new beginning and gift to herself and her child. Where was she going to go? Who could she tell?

She contacted her sister who agreed to let her live with her for a few months until she could find her own place.

She let her mother know her plans. (Her mother had been praying for the woman, also, and the news that she was leaving the monster gave her mother fresh hope for her daughter, "Thank you, God.")

She let her ex-husband know her plans. He was extremely supportive because he knew how the child felt about the boy. The child often said, "Daddy, I don't like Mommy's friend. He hurts me and yells a lot at me and Mommy. I hate him."

She and her child just needed to make it through one last weekend with the boy. Just one. And it would be a weekend to remember for everyone involved.

Part 20

Prelude to a Rage

As the eve of her birthday approached, the woman methodically prepared her exit. She secretly packed a small bag of clothes along with cash and important documents, identification cards, bank statements (her own), and passport. She put this bag in the trunk of her car and magnetically attached a spare key behind the left front wheel. She wasn't taking the chance of being kicked out of her home with nothing again.

The woman arranged for the child's father to pick him up after dinner on the eve of the woman's birthday. The woman wanted to be alone when she told the boy she was leaving him. (The best defense the woman had to protect herself from any physical harm was the lie that she was still pregnant. She felt certain that the boy wouldn't hurt her once she told him she was leaving, knowing she was carrying his baby. She wasn't completely certain, however, what other retaliatory actions he could and would take.)

The eve of her birthday came. While the boy practiced his keyboard pounding, the woman read and played with her son. She prepared a simple meal of chicken and rice, and they all sat down to eat. Within a few moments of starting their meal, the child began frantically waving his arms in the air without saying anything. A piece of the chicken was lodged in his throat. The boy screamed in the woman's direction, "What is wrong with him?! Can't you control him? He's so dramatic." The woman jumped up from her seat and grabbed the child from behind and lifted gently. The small piece of barely chewed chicken flew out onto his plate. The child simply cried in shock and fear.

The woman rubbed the child's chest and assured him everything would be fine. She asked him to drink some water and finish his dinner. But the child was too afraid to chew and swallow the chicken or the rice. So, the woman served him yogurt, something smooth and soothing.

The boy rolled his eyes at the child and called him a baby and said, "You were faking. You just wanted to have yogurt. You are such a little baby." The child, by now tired of defending himself against the boy's name calling, stuck his tongue out at the boy. The woman tried to finish her dinner. It took everything in her not to throw the remaining chicken and rice in the boy's face. Her anger had reached its boiling point. She was so disgusted by the boy's cruelty that she couldn't even look at his ugly face, his ugly distorted face.

The child's father arrived. "Finally," the woman whispered to herself. "Now it's my turn to leave."

Part 21

The Rage Begins

The woman kissed her child goodbye and watched as he walked to his father's car. Snow began falling, and she prayed it would stop soon.

Back inside, the boy asked the woman, "So, what did your fat ex-husband have to say?" The woman ignored him. The boy asked again. The woman continued to ignore him and walked into her bedroom, their bedroom, to relax. The boy followed her and asked again, louder this time. The woman looked up at him and said, "It's none of your business."

The boy did not like this response and lunged at the woman as she sat on the bed. He screamed in her face, "Get the FUCK out of MY house, you fucking WHORE!!" The woman calmly rested her head on the propped pillow behind her, reached for her book, and looked up at the boy with an expression of disgust.

Realizing she wasn't going to budge, the boy grabbed her by her shoulders and shook her screaming, "You fucking whore! Did you hear me? Get the FUCK out of MY house, or I'll call the police."

The woman looked at his grip and then into his eyes and said, "Call the police. What are they going to do? They'll see quickly that I live here and that a child, my son, lives here, too." Then she lost her calm and shouted, "You are a FUCKING cocksucker! I hate you!"

The boy shook her more. The woman tried to reach under the mattress for the bread knife she had hidden there weeks before. (Yes, a bread knife. It was the only knife the boy wouldn't have missed from the kitchen.) She wasn't going to let this monster get away with this, not this time. She was ready to fight and kill him if she needed to. But her reach was cut short by his grip. He let go after a minute or so and stood at the foot of the bed just staring at her and shaking his head.

The woman broke her silence again and said, "I'm moving out. I am leaving. I can't do this anymore."

The boy screamed, "Great! You never loved me anyhow, you fucking whore."

The woman had heard 'whore' come out of his mouth so many times that it meant nothing to her except hate. She stood to put on her shoes, and the boy pushed her back to the bed. She looked up at him, and he was crying.

"I'm sorry; I'm sorry. Please don't leave me. I'll stop. I can get better."

How many times had the woman heard these same pleading words before? She wasn't feeding into his crocodile tears this time. Instead, she ignored him and attempted to get up again. The boy pushed her back down. His tears had quickly dried and he screamed, "You are so selfish! You're a selfish whore who only cares about herself. All I ever wanted was for you to love me and NEED me. But you're nothing but a whore."

(Jesus! Is 'whore' the best he can do?)

The woman remained seated on the bed, crossed her arms in front of her, and sighed deeply and said, "You can't hurt me anymore. I am leaving and there is NOTHING you can do about it."

The boy smirked and said, "Haha! You think so? I can take that baby from you so you will NEVER see it, ever. What judge would allow a drunk to raise a child? What judge would allow a sick and mentally deranged woman to raise a child? You will NEVER get the chance to even hold that baby in your arms, you fucking whore!"

The woman just stared defiantly into his eyes. She surveyed the room for something, anything that she might be able to grab quickly to knock him out. He wasn't going to let her off the bed without a struggle.

But she was too tired to fight. She curled up on the bed as if to fall to sleep. Surprisingly, the boy left the room. The woman listened keenly to his footsteps and determined he was taking his dog out for a walk. The woman heard him fumble with the bowl of keys by the door.

Then the front door slammed. The woman looked out the bedroom window. Through the falling snow, she could see the boy get into her car and move it to the back of the driveway behind the house. In an instant, her hope of leaving on this night was gone.

Part 22

The Escape

Before the boy made it back inside the house, the woman slipped on her shoes and grabbed the bread knife under the mattress, tucking it into the back of her pants.

Upon entering, the boy yelled, "Go ahead and leave now, if you can. I can change the combination on the door (controlling much?) when you leave and you'll never get back inside MY house EVER again." (Pfft! Just what the woman wanted and knew he'd say. So predictable in his evilness.)

The woman walked to the coat closet. The boy blocked her, crying, "Don't do this. You can't do this. Besides, where will you go? You'll need to sell your car to be able to pay rent anywhere. You can't make it on your own. If you leave, you'll be begging me to let you back."

Instead of trying to push and fight her way to the closet behind him, the woman sat down on the sofa staring into nothingness and waited for him to leave. But he just stood in front of her with his hands crossed, staring at her and trying to intimidate her into staying. The woman's entire being was shaking from the inside out. She was angry but didn't want to express it. She just wanted the craziness to stop. She knew if she said anything, cried, smiled, or showed any kind of emotion, the boy would be triggered to react violently. All she could do was sit back, close her eyes, and breathe.

She imagined she was somewhere else. Somewhere safe and warm and familiar. She was anxious. She imagined pulling the knife from behind her back and plunging it into his gut. She despised the boy THAT much. But she thought of her son and the rest of her family who loved her. She wasn't going to let the boy destroy her. She wasn't going to succumb to his evil. (After all, it's what sociopaths try to do: project the evil onto victims so the victims feel and act like the evildoers.)

Finally, after what seemed like hours, the boy walked away and took his dog out into the snow for a walk, grabbing the woman's car keys on his way out the door. She watched through the window as the boy and his dog moved further and further down the street. Her courage soared quickly, and she raced out the back door through the snowy yard to her car. Her spare keys were still attached to the underside by the front wheel.

The falling snow made the evening eerily quiet around her. She got inside, put the key into the ignition, and slowly pulled away, easier than she had hoped through the mounting snow. The boy and his dog were nowhere in sight.

Part 23

The Aftermath

A lot has happened in the eighteen (18) months since the woman escaped the boy's insidious and evil abuse. How does someone move on from such trauma? How does someone move on from the pain? How does someone forgive such evil? How was the child impacted? Does the woman speak to the boy now? How does she feel about the boy today? Did the boy face any consequences for what he did? Does the boy acknowledge his part in the end of their relationship? Does the boy have a new victim he's priming?

Like sharing the story, the answers to these questions will take time to gather and write. The struggle is ongoing. Luckily, the child no longer remembers the boy's name or the name of the boy's dog. The boy remains "the one who shall remain nameless" in the woman's home. The woman is happily married to her son's father who helps her daily to put the pieces of her spirit back together. The woman has forgiven herself for putting her son in such danger but remains unable to forgive the boy. After all, in order to forgive the boy, doesn't the boy need to acknowledge that he behaved badly in the first place? Like the good narcissistic sociopath he is, the boy takes no accountability. Everything the woman got, she deserved. She didn't love him the way he NEEDED to be loved, remember?

Confidential sources have revealed to the woman that the boy continues to lure and abuse new victims. His family continues to say nothing, and the boy continues to repeat the same patterns. This sociopath, this boy, frolics blissfully along believing he is superior and untouchable. And he will continue wreaking havoc on the lives of everyone he touches because no one wants to be bothered to even challenge him anymore. No one believes stopping him is worth the effort.

But the woman believes differently. Stopping him may save someone's life one day. Stopping him may save a child's innocence one day. Stopping him may bring inner peace to the many he has caused suffering. But stopping him how? With words? That's what the woman hopes this story will accomplish. Maybe one day he will recognize he has a serious personality disorder, which is why he can't establish a single stable relationship to save his life. But then again, he's a sociopath, and sociopath's are incapable of true introspection. He won't stop until he stops. Simple. Sad. True.

Letter to The Boy

To The Boy,

Everyone is onto you. We know what you are and, more importantly, what you are not. You are NOT a good person. You are NOT beautiful. You are NOT a friend to anyone. You use words to hurt, ridicule and tear down. You hide behind a mask of superiority, but we all see it and know it's false. You always NEED to win. But do you?

You are a sad, soulless mass. You pick on children. You treat waiters and waitresses like garbage. You jump in line claiming you were there first. You act like an infant, yet claim to be above reproach.

You point out everyone else's flaws but your own. You criticize the clothes and accessories people wear (as if stuff really matters). You pretend to have feelings, but what you really do is imitate what you BELIEVE are feelings. You're an actor and a bad one.

Until you realize that you are flawed, you will forever be flawed and without true friends. The people in your life just tolerate you because they feel pity for you. (But that's what you want, right?)

I have no pity for you. I wish you could see yourself for what you truly are and maybe save yourself from yourself before it's too late. Don't fool another woman into falling in love with you. Don't idolize her and then destroy her like you have done with so many others. Focus on finding your soul instead of your soul mate, okay?

Who are you, boy? What makes you happy? What do you want to learn? What do you want to see? Who do you want to become? Have you ever asked yourself these questions? It can't be enough just to be what you are today: an empty shell of a person with no identity.

Turn off your television, your computer, and your anger. Talk to yourself for a change. Take a good look in the mirror and ask yourself, "If I died today, who would care?" And answer that question honestly. It will hurt, especially if you're honest. It's supposed to hurt.

Life is simple. You've made your life complicated and dark, along with the lives of those you've trapped in the dungeon with you. Free them. Free yourself. Find peace. Then discover what has eluded you your entire life ~ LIFE. LOVE. LAUGHTER. LONGING.

Signed,
The Woman

Afterward
Putting an End to Domestic Violence and Intimate Partner Abuse

Domestic violence/intimate partner abuse is a growing and often ignored epidemic in the United States. Most victims will never be heard because they are too scared, too ashamed, or already dead at the hands of their abuser. Many of these victims (and those who do survive) suffer depression, anxiety and post-traumatic stress disorder (PTSD). Some may become suicidal or even homicidal.

According to a 2000 study by the Centers for Disease Control and Prevention and The National Institute of Justice, one in four women (25%) has experienced domestic violence in her lifetime. According to a 2010 survey, one in seven men experienced severe physical violence by an intimate partner. A related 2006 study by the Allstate Foundation determined that nearly three out of four (74%) of Americans personally know someone who has been a victim of domestic violence.

If this many people are affected by domestic violence/intimate partner abuse, why isn't anyone talking about it? Are you talking about it? It is not a subject we discuss in the break room at the office or on the sidelines of soccer games. As enormous as the problem is, why not? It could be because most of us consider the subject too personal and intimate to discuss with strangers or casual acquaintances. Or maybe we don't discuss it because we really don't understand what it is.

The website for The National Domestic Violence Hotline defines domestic violence:

- Domestic violence can be defined as a pattern of behavior in any relationship that is used to gain or maintain power and control over an intimate partner.
- Abuse is physical, sexual, emotional, economic or psychological actions or threats of actions that influence another person. This includes any behaviors that frighten, intimidate, terrorize, manipulate, hurt, humiliate, blame, injure or wound someone.
- Domestic violence can happen to anyone of any race, age, sexual orientation, religion or gender. It can happen to couples who are married, living together or who are dating. Domestic violence affects people of all socioeconomic backgrounds and education levels (http://www.thehotline.org/, retrieved August 20, 2012).

Few studies have been conducted to support the connection between personality disorders and domestic violence/intimate partner abuse, because most victims are too ashamed to admit they were abused/are being abused and often think they did/are doing something to cause the abuse. Victims are silenced by their own fears of being revictimized, making breakthroughs in research and understanding difficult if not impossible. This lack of research hinders the jobs of law enforcement, mental health professionals, and social workers that desperately want to recognize the signs and know how to interact with victims more effectively.

I provided my story and hope others will be encouraged to share their own one day. Our pain and suffering may help others end their suffering sooner or allow such pain and suffering to be avoided completely.

Consider visiting my website and blog and participating in the Red Riding Hood Project this Halloween (and every Halloween to come) by dressing up in a red cape and hood. You can make your voice heard without even saying a word. You can bring hope to the silent sufferers who just want inner peace and to live a happy and long life free from abuse, fear, and control. Together we can put a stop to domestic violence/ intimate partner abuse.

Red Riding Hood Project (www.paularenee.wordpress.com/ red-riding-hood-project)

Escaping the Boy: My life with a Sociopath (www.storyofasociopath. com)

Cited Sources and Resources

National Domestic Violence Hotline
http://www.thehotline.org/
1-800-799-SAFE

BOOKS

Dangerous Liaisons: How to Recognize and Escape from Psychopathic Seduction
Claudia Moscovici (2011)

How to Save Your Daughter's Life: Straight Talk for Parents from America's Top Criminal Profiler
Pat Brown (2012)

Malignant Self-Love: Narcissism Revisited
Sam Vaknin (2001)

Red Flags of Love Fraud: 10 Signs You're Dating a Sociopath
Donna Andersen (2012)

The Sociopath Next Door
Martha Stout, Ph.D. (2006)

Without Conscience: The Disturbing World of the Psychopaths Among Us
Robert D. Hare, Ph.D (1999)

WEBSITES

www.storyofasociopath.com—Official website for *Escaping the Boy: My life with a Sociopath*

www.facebook.com/escapingtheboy—Facebook page for *Escaping the Boy: My life with a Sociopath*

www.lovefraud.com—Beware the sociopath: No heart, no conscience, no remorse

www.ncadv.org—National Coalition Against Domestic Violence

www.nomore.org—NO MORE is spotlighting an invisible problem in a whole new way.

www.paularenee.wordpress.com/red-riding-hood-project—Red Riding Hood Project

BLOGS

www.onemomsbattle.com—One Mom's Battle: Narcissism and Family Court

www.paularenee.wordpress.com—Paula's Pontifications: Life, Love, Laughter, Longing

www.psychopathyawareness.wordpress.com—Claudia Moscovici's blog on the subject

About the Author

Paula Carrasquillo lives and works in the Washington, D.C. area. She loves to read and practices Bikram yoga for her physical and emotional well being. She earned an M.A. in communication and adult education from Regis University in Denver, Colorado and her bachelor's in English from Frostburg State University in Frostburg, Maryland.

Paula has worked with the at-risk population as a curriculum developer and an educator teaching GED, ESL, and Life Skills courses. She currently works as a web and content analyst for a Federal contractor. She also writes a weekly column for The Washington Times online Communities, Living Inside Out Loud.

Paula is currently working on her next book to be released in early 2013.

Keep up with the author and visit her site: www.paulareneereeves.com.

CPSIA information can be obtained at www.ICGtesting.com
Printed in the USA
BVOW030841080513

320181BV00003B/712/P